Leading in the Digital Age

Disruption, Transformation, Data,

Cybersecurity, Artificial Intelligence

First Edition

Thomas Cowan

Table of Contents

Chapter 1 – A Letter to the CEO

You are likely a CEO, or maybe a CIO, CTO, CFO, or other C-Suite leader. You may be on a Board of Directors. You may be a divisional or functional leader, manager, or supervisor.

Regardless of where you sit, you need to deal with the emerging technologies in your job on a daily basis – and not just the technologies themselves, but also the societal, organizational, and ethical issues surrounding them.

I've been in your position, as a CEO who has built companies, a Board member for technology start-ups, and a manager trying to run a business in the face of the disruption and transformation that technology can create. Now, at Columbia University's Center for Technology Management, I work with leaders to develop and implement the decisions, plans, and strategies related to technology and the complications of that environment. I've been thinking deeply about leadership in an age of rapid technological change and its accompanying disruption, and want to share my thinking with you.

This short book presents an overview of my current thinking about the environment we are living in and the challenges, opportunities, and risks we face. I want to illuminate the situation and lay the groundwork for you as you think through your strategies, plans, and execution.

This is an exciting time for the CEO, entrepreneur, and technologist. My job is to help you navigate these murky but exciting waters.

Chapter 2 – Setting the Context

It is essential in everything we do to think in terms of both how we execute and how we keep our minds open to creativity. I like this quote from Albert Einstein.

"Logic will get you from A to B. Imagination will take you everywhere."
– Albert Einstein

Einstein used his imagination in thought experiments, and then when he reached conclusions, he used logic to articulate the outcome.

I like to think in the same terms about the technology problems we're going to discuss. And not just the problems, but also the opportunities and the challenges of technology. The questions that I think are relevant have to do with digital disruption and transformation. Specifically, what do these terms mean in relation to technology? How do the terms differ? How do digital disruption and transformation affect what we do, how we do it, and how we live?

What can we do about it? Are there actions we should be taking in relation to these topics? How does disruption change how we operate, how we buy items, how we carry out routine activities? We'll answer these questions by looking at the various technologies that are prominent and interesting today.

When people ask me to give them an example of digital disruption, I talk about Uber. Before Uber, we took taxis: we randomly waited for taxis in New York City or any other major city. Taxi service did not exist everywhere. In many small towns, there may have been a random taxi or two, but not in my small town in Connecticut. Now, what Uber did was take existing technologies that are available to us all today, like GPS, cellular systems, credit card processing, access to the internet, and mobile applications.

Uber pulled these technologies together in a smart way, knit them together in a smart way, and then delivered a service based on the aggregation of existing technologies. Then they created a business model that enabled many people to act as taxis in the community they lived in. A simple idea: take existing technologies and put them together to serve a creative business model that matches those who want jobs with those who need transportation. This disrupted not just the taxi industry, but the transportation industry as a whole.

In general, I think disruption, which we'll define in detail in a bit, is a positive thing. I think, though, that we should always be vigilant about whether the side effects of disruption are positive or negative – and if they are negative, whether they warrant action on our part.

For instance, in the past, when I needed cash, I went to my bank – in my local community – and asked a teller to withdraw money from my account. That was somebody's job, to help me access my cash. Now, banks have replaced that teller with an ATM machine, and I can go pretty much anywhere and withdraw money from my bank account, without ever going to my bank. In fact, I haven't been to my bank in years.

ATMs are a good disruption because they make my life better. I like being able to go almost anywhere in the world and get cash. But there is a negative: they take away people's jobs.

The question then becomes: Should we do something about it? And if so, what? Should we work to find a better position for those people who were displaced in their jobs, help them with their skills, and place them at a higher-level function within the organization? And the answer, of course, is "yes."

Let's get more relevant and more specific here: I rarely use ATMs anymore because Apple Pay on my Apple Watch serves me pretty well in paying for things where I used to use cash or a credit card. I imagine many of you do the same. So even the disruption of the ATM has now been disrupted by another smart business model, again enabled by technology.

The effects of disruption fall on three major groups: (1) large organizations; (2) the entrepreneurial community; and (3) individuals in terms of how we experience these disruptions and then go on to live our lives.

Let's start looking at some specific technologies. I'm going to start by looking at the technology that is the furthest out in my judgment: artificial intelligence (AI). An increasing number of people believe that artificial intelligence will replace human beings in the workplace. Not just replace them through automation, as in the ATM example, but replace all humans in the workplace through AI. Some people take it even further than that and say that AI will replace human beings in general. They believe that AI will develop super-human capabilities, meaning capabilities beyond what humans can do, and will act on these capabilities on its own. As a result, we as human beings will be at the mercy of these AIs.

If you really want to scare yourself, you can read a couple of books on this topic. You may want to try Ray Kurzweil's *The Singularity is Near*, which was published in 2005 and still is viable today. Or better yet, try Nick Bostrom's *Superintelligence*, which was published in 2015. But be aware that these books do not put your mind to rest. Bostrom offers a lot of solutions, solutions he thinks are viable for the issues he raises, but they're not comforting. I would say Bostrom is reasonably balanced in that he spends a lot of time talking about the good aspects of AI.

Another book, published in 2017, maybe the place to start in your reading: *Life 3.0* by MIT professor Max Tegmark. He does an incredible job of describing our development as human beings, and the parallel development of artificial intelligence against our development as humans, and what the resulting environment will be like. He is a bit more optimistic. I share that optimism. I think both Tegmark and I (and I don't want to put myself in Tegmark's company by any stretch) believe that technology adds enormous benefits to our everyday lives, has done so for many centuries, and will continue to do so in the future. Just as we figured out how to control the power of technology up until now, we will figure out how to control its power in the future. We just have to be diligent about it.

Tegmark makes the point, and I fully agree, that our job is to stay ahead of the advancement of technology. As long as we stay ahead of its advancement, we are okay. But the day we let ourselves lag behind its advancement will be the day we will have a lot of work to do to catch up, if even possible.

Here's an example some of you may remember: the Y2K issue at the change of the century, from 1999 to 2000. That change from the number 1999 to the number 2000 was concerning to many technologists. The fear was that existing enterprise systems – corporate systems such as financial systems, logistic systems, the stock exchange, etc. – could not deal with the "2" instead of the "1" as the starting digit of the year wherever a date was required in the system.

In fact, we had very little trouble with it. We anticipated it, and spent at least a year, if not more, doubling down, making sure the systems could accommodate the change. And they did: we crossed over from 1999 to 2000 pretty much unscathed.

The Y2K issue became personal for me. I was working at IBM at the time, but left partly because I found myself thinking, "This is crazy – to still be working on these old systems that have problems like this. Maybe it's time to go out and start working on new systems that incorporate more forward thinking."

So, I left IBM and entered the entrepreneurial ranks to build businesses, because I saw the opportunities into the 2000s versus what we were dealing with in the 1990s. Technology became a motivator for me, the reason for becoming an entrepreneur, to build businesses, to look for opportunities created by technology in the face of an apparent disruption.

To make sense of the issues we are facing today, which we've created by the use of technology, it might be helpful to think in a broader sense, a historical context.

Humans have gone through a number of sweeping societal changes, all of which have affected what we do, how we do it, and how we live. Let's go through some of these changes to see if they can help us put what is going on today into a helpful context.

Chapter 3 – A Historical Perspective

Let's start with the Agricultural Age, perhaps the first sweeping societal change we as human beings lived through. This change is commonly referred to as the Agricultural Revolution. It occurred in multiple waves at different times across the globe. It changed the way we grew things, which in turn changed how we lived.

Many positives came out of this age. We learned how to farm, to grow food for ourselves rather than just wait for nature to present it to us. A natural follow-on benefit was the resulting division of labor. We no longer had to all be hunter-gatherers to maintain our lives, or live apart from one another because we needed enough room to hunt and gather food and water to live. We could now divide the labor and work collaboratively to supply ourselves with food and water.

Another positive from this division of labor was that we could now live in social collectives, such as villages and later towns and cities. And as people started to see the benefits from this division of labor, they began to collect things, things that other people wanted. So, conflict began to develop over these possessions and the land that had become ever more important for farming.

These villages, towns, and cities enabled us to better defend ourselves against conflict. We had learned the benefit of collective defense before the Agricultural Age, but living in collectives gave us an added improvement in defense.

This age also saw the beginning of more extensive trade, or what we today think of as business. And this trade led to the origins of wealth creation.

But a significant side effect began to emerge from these changes – disease. Disease was an adverse side effect of living together in these villages, towns, and cities. There were a lot of reasons for this, but a significant cause was not properly disposing of waste. As we know from history, life was not a very pleasant experience for a lot of people for a long time, with waste running down streets. It was not only unpleasant; the waste created a disease factory for these communities.

The Industrial Age (or Industrial Revolution) was the second sweeping societal change we saw. Where the Agricultural Age was about how we grew things, the Industrial Age was about how we made things, and consequently, it changed what we made and how we lived.

Another important aspect of this age was that wealth started to be created in significant ways, in ways that had not been seen before. Improvements in productivity drove this wealth-creation. Until then, society could only do what a human could do. But with the productivity improvements of the Industrial Age, we figured out how to do more than a single human being could do. This was enabled by the use of very early technologies to create and use machines. We began putting these machines into the early incarnations of factories, and the use of those machines then drove productivity.

This early use of machines in factories was seen mostly in the textile industry in England, and then in America, where it flourished mainly in the southern areas. These were the early stages of what we would today think of as automation. People were using machines to automate tasks to enable humans to do more than they could do on their own, and in less time.

An acute side effect began to emerge, though, and that was worker health and safety. This problem was caused by machine pollution and unsafe working areas and practices inside the factory.

Just as we worked to solve the disease issues of the Agricultural Age, we worked through and began solving the problems of worker health, safety, and exploitation. But, unfortunately, the adverse effects of both ages still exist in a number of the less well-developed societies around the world today.

How does this historical review help us understand the issues we're facing today with technology? Perhaps the lesson we can draw from this history is to anticipate. It may have been difficult to anticipate the adverse side effects of the Agricultural Age, or the Industrial Age, but I do wonder about that.

If we could have stood in those streets or watched what was going on in those factories, could we have anticipated the problems? I would like to think we could have, but the context and experience of today's world makes it seem much easier to anticipate than it likely would have been. Despite our lack of context and knowledge, though, I think we should always try.

I think we should consciously anticipate the negative effects of what we are doing and how we live. The positives are there for all to see. And as an entrepreneur and business builder, I'm constantly thinking of how to exploit these positives with products and business models.

But trying to anticipate the emerging negatives also offers opportunity – opportunity for both the entrepreneur and the large company to benefit society. I think that, as a good entrepreneur or corporate intrapreneur, it is worth our while spending at least part of our creative thinking on the emerging negatives and the opportunities they offer.

I think it wise to try to anticipate these consequential negatives and head them off, rather than have them occur in some significant way. When they do occur, which is what has mostly happened to us in the past, we have had to spend enormous amounts of resources and effort trying to solve them, likely much more than if we had anticipated and dealt with them earlier. And if you read Max Tegmark's book *Life 3.0*, mentioned earlier, you can see that he is thinking along these same lines.

Chapter 4 – Disruption & Transformation

Disruption

The common theme we saw in both the Agricultural Age and the Industrial Age was a significant disruption – a disruption that markedly changed what we did, how we did things, and how we lived. So, I think it would be helpful to go through the fundamentals of disruption to try to make sense of the issues we're facing today with technology. This is especially true if we are taking a balanced view of the potential positives and negatives while looking for opportunity.

Let's start by defining Disruption. "Disruption" in the context we are using here – the context of technology – is a significant change. It is a change that is significant enough to materially reshape what we do, how we do things, and how we live.

You can tell that I'm using three data points to help us understand if a change is significant, a change to: (1) what we do, (2) how we do things, and (3) how we live. I know of no measures that easily define disruption, so I've adopted these.

If something changes what we do, how we do things, and how we live, I think it qualifies as a disruption. And these measures conform well to our definition of the Agricultural Age and Industrial Age as significant disruptions. As we discussed before, both ages changed what humans did, how they did things, and how they lived.

So, one way to determine if something is a disruption is to ask if it changes what you do, how you do things, and how you live. But to go deeper to answer the question as to whether something is a business disruption, a second question to ask is whether something changed a market, business model, or organization.

Let's take a simple example that most of us can relate to. Let's take the case of the teller and the ATM. I would argue that the change caused by the ATM may not have disrupted a market, but it certainly disrupted a business model. The reason I think it did not disrupt a market is that it did not materially change whether we did business with banks. Had the disruption taken us away from doing business with banks and moved us to something else, that would have qualified as a disruption to the market.

But the change from tellers to ATMs did change how banks did business with us. The business model of retail banks no longer called for you to interact with a human being for specific tasks, such as making deposits or withdrawing cash from your account. That's a business model change. The introduction of ATMs across the banking sector--worldwide--constituted a change in the business model of retail banking.

And why was that change adopted by banking customers and sustained over a period of time? Retail banking customers judged that ATMs gave them a better experience. And why did the organization adopt the ATM change? Retail banks judged that it was a more efficient process, increasing productivity and lowering costs. (I will add that banks judged that their retail customers would have a better banking experience using ATMs, but not everyone would agree with that.)

A second term worth defining in our context of technology is Digital Disruption. "Digital Disruption" is where a significant change occurs with the use of data – data – plus all the things you need to make data useful: data management systems and the networks that connect these systems to themselves and human beings.

A simple example of digital disruption is fantasy sports gaming. You can play a game like fantasy football, using data on how each player has played in the past. And you play this game through a device that connects to a network where the game resides. Instead of you having to research each player's historical performance, the game has already collected the data for you. And instead of you playing this game with only people you are physically near, you can play against anyone connected to the network from around the world.

All this is possible because of the use of data and connectivity. For the gamer, it has changed what you do, how you do it, and perhaps if you are in the gaming industry, how you live! This can be thought of as a market disruption – to the gaming industry – driven by data and connectivity. (I apologize to all those gaming enthusiasts out there – I am sure that I did not do this subject its full justice.)

I like to use the term "disruption" for something that causes change – something that disturbs, upsets, or interferes with things as they are. We saw examples of this with the macro disruptions of the Agricultural Age and Industrial Age. And we've seen a disruption of a market with fantasy sports gaming and a disruption of a business model with retail banking ATMs.

Transformation

Another term worth defining is Transformation. I like to think of "Transformation" as rebuilding something -- your organization, a business model, or a market. It is helpful to think of disruption as throwing an aspect of chaos into the mix, while transformation is the act of rebuilding after the disturbance.

To take this further, you can rebuild something voluntarily, or you can rebuild something in response to disruption. You can wait and have some disruption create an element of chaos in your organization, business model, or organization. And then you can do one of two things: (1) you can react and respond to that disruption; or (2) you can be proactive and transform in anticipation of a disruption.

There is a third option that many of my entrepreneurial colleagues would like to think they could do – be the disruptor, the one with the idea who disrupts a market or industry. I would like to think there are a lot of people like Steve Jobs, Bill Gates, and Elon Musk around, but I just don't think there are. It is more likely that most of us are disrupting business models, organizations, and functions.

Another example of disruption is Airbnb. Airbnb saw what Uber did to the taxi industry and said, "We could take that same business model and change how the hotel and rental property market works." They saw the disruption Uber created and decided to apply it to a different market.

So, what does that have to do with transformation? Let's take this example a little further. What if you were one of the large global hotel chains? And what if you had taken the Uber model and created your own Airbnb? Before Airbnb emerged, you set up a division of your company or a separate company (usually the more successful approach) to match Airbnb. You would have been on the path to do two things: (1) disrupt the market for rental accommodations, and (2) transform your organization in the process.

A more complex example is IBM. IBM disrupted the technology market multiple times and was often thought of as the leader in various aspects of technology over its long history. But when it was recently disrupted, IBM did not respond well, in my judgment.

(Full disclosure here, I started my business career at IBM and am somewhat biased in that I still love the company to this day. It was a wonderful training ground, and I just hope I contributed as much to them as they have given me.)

The market disruption IBM experienced was cloud computing. IBM has had many years of difficulty finding its footing with this disruption. During this time, of course, IBM kept researching and developing outstanding technology, but it was the conversion that was lacking.

What I mean by "conversion" is converting these technologies into new products and services that make up a significant part of their revenue and profit results. You may be creating great technology, but without revenue and profit conversion, these technologies lack the substance of business results.

Conversion is one of the most critical parts of what great entrepreneurs and organizational intrapreneurs do. For growth reasons, they may return all profits (and maybe more) into investments in the growth engine, but the conversion is there – it is just a different strategy – a strategy of growth versus profit. Regardless, new products and services make up a significant part of the revenue of the company, demonstrating conversion.

So where is IBM today? It has made a bet on artificial intelligence as the future of its company – or at least that is how it appears from the outside. You probably know that IBM has branded its artificial intelligence Watson, and has spent a great deal on advertising that name. Watson, then called Deep Blue, beat Gary Kasparov in chess in 1997, and by 2010 regularly beat humans at Jeopardy!.

After being disrupted by cloud computing and SaaS software delivery, IBM is now rebuilding and transforming the company on the back of AI. They are looking to convert all the great technology innovation in AI they are doing around the world in their research labs into products and services that contribute significantly to their revenue and profit growth.

A counterargument might be that IBM is too early. Is there enough commercial usefulness of AI to bet your business on it today? I think the jury is still out on that, but IBM does have my admiration for picking AI. As we'll discover when we discuss AI in more detail, I think AI is the enabling technology of the future. It will become part of everything we do – our lives, our work, and how we live. IBM appears to be anticipating a potential disruption from AI and is either trying to, best case, be the disruptor, or, worst case, transform the business to meet it. It's a big bet, but I like the direction they are heading.

Just remember real disruptors – like Apple, Google, and Uber – want to disrupt your business through changing the market and hoping you are not good enough or quick enough to transform your business to match their disruption. That is their bet. And that is the IBM bet with AI.

Chapter 5 – A Digital Platform

What are we seeing with disruptions today? Are we seeing a series of functional and organizational disruptions, or are we seeing business model and market disruptions? We are seeing all of the above. And they are happening in almost every single market.

One could argue that Jeff Bezos at Amazon is attempting disruption in a number of markets. He first disrupted retail bookselling, then retail product selling, and now he's trying to disrupt the world of groceries (with Whole Foods) and news and journalism (with The Washington Post).

But are we seeing a macro disruption – an extraordinary disruption – bigger than any particular market, or business, or business model – one akin to the Industrial Age or Agricultural Age?

One of the ways to untangle this is to look at some of the indicators or symptoms that we see in the market to determine whether some extraordinary disruption is occurring.

Over the past few years, technology has created a Digital Platform – you could call it a digital foundation – and we have placed our organizations, and even our individual lives, on top of this platform.

The idea is that you are no longer, for example, a hospital system. You are an organization running a hospital system on top of a digital platform.

What this makes clear is that every organization has become, or is quickly becoming, a digital organization.

We run our businesses and organizations, and our lives, on top of this digital platform.

I believe most organizations today would have a difficult time running their business without that digital platform.

And I imagine that most of us in our society today, especially in the developed societies, would have a difficult time living our lives as we have come to know them, without that digital platform.

We have changed our businesses, organizations, and lives so much to depend on the ability to access information instantly, instantly communicate, and continuously feed those information and communication systems we have built – the digital platform.

Dealing with this change in how we run our businesses and live our lives requires a shift in thinking, especially concerning the strategies and plans we employ, and the actions we and our employees carry out.

It also creates a widening gap between those who are comfortable with these changes and those who are not comfortable and are not adjusting their thinking. Anecdotal information would suggest that this gap will continue to widen.

Chapter 6 – Data & Access

What's going on here? And how did this happen? What caused it?

I think two things are going on here – Data and Access. Let's take that apart.

Data

Data now seems to be coming from almost everywhere, and many predict data will continue to multiply in growth well into the 2020s. And I'm excluding scientific data here, which is growing even faster than non-scientific data. (The growth in scientific data is driven, in large part, by our space telescopes and antennas that are continuously collecting cosmological data.)

Beyond our existing sources of data, new markets of data are emerging. The Internet of Things (IoT) and edge computing are just two examples of new markets that are heavy in data collection. We are now collecting data from elevators, refrigerators, television sets, and even our cars. I can tell you where my car is parked, how much gas it has, and whether it's locked, even if I'm on the other side of the United States when I do it.

Access

The next thing we are seeing, beyond just the data, is an expansion of access to the data. You not only have the multiplication of data, but you also have the expansion of access to that data.

Some might be tempted to use the term "connectivity" here. I like the word "access" though, in that I think it more easily incorporates the important aspects here – being able to retrieve data from where it resides, use it, send the result to where it needs to go, and add entirely new data to the data store.

Systems

We have built large and complex systems that manage and manipulate data. These systems are becoming more prevalent and sophisticated. Examples of these systems are Procurement, Production, Distribution, Accounting, HR, Corporate Performance, Customer Service, Sales & Marketing, Business Intelligence, e-Commerce, Asset Management ... I could keep going here. And these are just the traditional ERP-like systems. To that, we are now adding Robotics and Artificial Intelligence to the list. (I am leaving big data and data analytics systems off the list. I think of them as part of Business Intelligence (BI) systems. One could argue that they will be incorporated into all AI systems in the future.)

Networks

We have built networks that are enabling broad access to these systems and data. The most obvious one is the Internet, which continues to grow in its reach and access points, including wi-fi networks. And then there is the cellular network that, through its corresponding data function, extends the network reach. So, we have gone beyond wires and now added the airwaves.

The basic point here is that, not only do you have immense growth of data, you also have immense growth of access.

And just as there is a lot of potential growth left in data, so it is with access. (Just come out to my home in Arizona, head into the desert for a while, and you will lose access to networks, and consequently data, pretty fast! We haven't talked about how GPS and satellite communications/radio play into all this, but I imagine we will in the next edition of this book.)

Chapter 7 – Digital Platform – Positives & Negatives

We've been discussing the attributes of data & access, but what about the positives and negatives?

Much as we did with the historical discussion of the positives and negatives of the Agricultural and Industrial Ages, let's look at the benefits and downsides of data & access.

Data & Access

To understand the positives and negatives of data & access, let's go to the workplace.

Positives

The more data & access our workforce has to the right information – along with systems and tools to put that data into the context of their jobs – the more valuable data & access are to them and the organization. It is most likely how the organization builds its value.

It is also important to understand that the same data & access that is valuable to your workforce, is valuable to a bad actor – someone wanting to do damage to your organization.

And don't be fooled by the shortness of this section – the positives of data & access are clear and immensely valuable.

Data & access are vital to the functioning of the organization today, but can also be its most serious threat.

Some of the most significant, most expensive and damaging cyber breaches were at Sony, FedEx, Equifax, Merck, Maersk. The damage done to those organizations is substantial. (Unfortunately, I could keep going with this list of large and well-known global organizations.)

Plus, the costs to these organizations of their cyber breaches were so significant, they threatened the very existence of their organizations – and when I say that, I don't mean just financially, with a lot of zeros behind the numbers, but also the damage to the confidence of their customers, partners, suppliers, and investors.

Let's go a bit deeper into cyber attacks and breaches because they are the most damaging negative aspect of data & access at the moment.

Equifax Example

Take Equifax for example, Equifax is in the business of credit reporting. It had a major breach, as most people know, where a significant amount of the financial (and personal) information Equifax had collected on people was copied and is now available for bad actors to use.

Let's examine this a little closer. As with me, I doubt Equifax ever came to you and said: "Can I put your information in my company's database?" They didn't have to. They were able to collect data on us from banks and credit card companies and create files on us.

But they never came to us and asked if they could maintain a file on us with that data. Now, most of us didn't do anything about it, because it was helpful to us. It helped us when we wanted a credit card, or a car loan, or a mortgage.

But there was never a formal agreement between Equifax and us. We never asked "What information are you going to collect? Who's going to own it within your organization? How are you going to use it? When do you decide that it's no longer useful and purge it? How are you going to store it? Where are you going to store it? How long are you going to store it?" And finally, "How well is it protected? What kind of security are you going to put around that data to make sure that it's not at risk and doesn't cause me problems in the future?"

We never had an agreement between us, based on an analytic framework that defined

Collection, Use, Storage, and Security. (This CUSS framework is the one we are using in our work at the moment.)

Yet, Equifax was attacked and breached, and now all the information they had on us is available to the public – available if you know how to access it on the dark web.

It's worth taking a moment to define the terms here – attack and breach. An "attack" is trying to get into systems. A "breach" is where you have gotten into the system. There are many more attacks than breaches.

Thousands of breaches occur every day. An instructive thing to do is ask any CIO, CTO or CISO (Chief Information Security Officer) of any major corporation, how many cyber-attacks they have in any one day. You would be astounded at the number. It has a lot of zeros.

Bad actors are attacking data and information, and they're doing it through the systems and networks we have created. They are attacking the digital platform we have built – the digital foundation we are running our businesses on and living our lives on.

I don't need to give you multiple examples here – let's just use a personal perspective. All we have to do is look at how many of our passwords have been exposed, or when our credit cards have been inappropriately used, or our identity stolen.

These can be incredibly difficult situations to work through and materially affect how we live our lives.

Motivations

Bad actor motivations are becoming much more sophisticated and complex.

It started years ago with young hackers who found it fun to try to hack into the CIA, NSA, NRO, or any of the three-letter secret government organizations. It seemed as though they didn't want to do anything other than prove that they could perpetrate a breach. But then the motivations moved to creating chaos, then to creating problems, and then to creating damage. This has happened to social organizations, governments, and businesses.

And now motivations have moved to financial gain. It goes something like this, "If you want us to unlock your systems – because we just locked them down – pay us a million bucks in bitcoin, and we'll unlock them for you." (Taking the right action here is beyond the scope of what we are covering in this discussion, but these are serious situations that require serious consideration and professional help, both inside and outside the law enforcement community.)

Another disturbing motivation may be emerging – that of strategic gain. This goes beyond a bitcoin ransom as described above, and moves into taking some kind of strategic action – perhaps to gain market share. When a friend and I were discussing this over coffee one day about a year ago, it seemed like a long way from reality. Now I'm not so sure that's the case.

An example of this could play out like this: one competitor attacks another to gain market share. The attacker might be a bad actor company, in a country that is not your friend, that attacks you with the objective of doing damage to you to help themselves. You can imagine all kinds of permutations on this – government against company, government against market, company against company, company against market, etc.

Probably the best thing to do about this motivation is to take note of it and hope it takes a long time for the bad actors to get to this one.

Chapter 8 – Artificial Intelligence (Why are you bringing this up now?)

I think it's important to talk about two notable technology developments we see – robotics and artificial intelligence.

I realize this might seem like a big jump from data & access, the digital platform, and cybersecurity, but I promise there is a point to my madness. (For a hint, check out the section below.)

The Prime Technology of the Future

I'll break the news to you now – artificial Intelligence, in my view, is the prime technology of the future – the most important one we will have at our disposal going forward. So that's why including an overview of it here is vital to our objective of giving you a picture of the future technology landscape.

Robotics

Let's break ourselves away from the world of
cybersecurity – and all the other issues of the
day – and clear our mind by leaping to the
world of robotics.

Why do a lot of us have the idea that robots
are going to be the really bad actors? I think it
goes back to the Arnold Schwarzenegger days
of movies like Terminator.

Robots can have human-like characteristics –
human-like form and function. And because of
this form and function, they appear to have an
ability to do bad things in a human-like way –
they have arms and legs, a "brain.", and the
ability to move around, sometimes much
quicker than humans.

I think we know now, though, that you don't
need human-like form and function to do bad
things.

I want to take you back to 1968 and a movie called 2001: A Space Odyssey, an incredible movie by Stanley Kubrick. I realize this movie may have been made before many of you were born, but it was really ahead of its time.

In the movie, there is a computer named HAL. Those of us who went on to work at IBM had a pretty good laugh at the following inside joke – you can see the letter progression here – just move up the alphabet one letter each, and you convert HAL to IBM. And you'll also appreciate that now, 50 years later, IBM is focusing its strategy on the technology that enabled HAL. IBM is just calling it Watson instead – probably a good choice, the reasons for which will become clear in a moment.

HAL communicated through a camera, a speaker, and a microphone. You would think that would make HAL pretty harmless, but it did not. HAL had access to everything – all the data and systems.

He had access to every system in the space capsule – and I say 'he' because HAL had a male voice. HAL had access to every system that made everything work – or stop working – including life support systems.

So here you have this computer with a camera, a speaker, and a microphone, and access and data. To make matters worse, HAL used machine learning to develop the ability to simulate aspects of human consciousness, so that he could now simulate the way that humans analyzed emotions, dealt with emotions, and so forth.

There's a funny line in the movie where HAL says, "I know you're lying because your lips are moving."

I hope I have not ruined the movie for you, because it is worth seeing if you haven't. It is beautifully produced, acted, and the story has profound lessons.

Pull the Plug! (to Data & Access)

With HAL in mind, let's do a quick thought experiment – an Einstein thought experiment – using our imagination, much like Einstein did to solve his problems with physics. (Which I contend were much greater than this one!)

Let's consider a worst-case scenario. Let's consider an out-of-control AI – much like HAL.

The first question to ask is, what gives this AI its power to act?

Almost all the emergency measures that are envisioned by futurists to stop a runaway AI, involve stopping data and access – the old-fashioned "pull the plug."

But pull the plug in two ways – pull the plug to the data, and pull the plug to the access. It is almost universal that, again, this issue of data and access floats to the top.

So please keep data and access top of mind, because they apply as much to the values and perils of the workplace as they do to the runaway AI of tomorrow. It is how we deal with these issues of data and access going forward that will matter.

Defining AI

Let's explore AI a bit deeper. Not just because I love it, but because I think it is important, and will be important for the future.

Much like "disruption" and "transformation," the terms used in AI are casually used and misused. So let's define the terms of AI as best we can from this emerging technology. I think doing this will help us understand important aspects of the disruption we are living through today, where it appears to be going, and perhaps a little about what we should do about it.

But first – what is AI? And how does it differ from traditional computing? One way to look at it is that AI solves the problems Classical Computing is not good at. Classical computing is at its best when it can give you certain answers – arithmetic answers – 2+2 = 4. AI is used to give you predictive answers – those that do not have a certain outcome – what is the likelihood you have cancer.

Also, to get best performance, you run them on different computing systems – Classical Computing runs best on a CPU (central processing unit – standard PC) while AI runs best on a GPU (graphics processing unit – think video games). That right there should tell you the type of computing these two applications do is very different – certainty versus prediction.

So – to summarize – AI is best used when the problem is predictive, you can break the problem down into parts, and there is a lot of relevant data available. Keep this in mind as we proceed.

When defining the terms of AI, I think it's helpful to think of AI as having three aspects: (1) approaching human cognition; (2) reaching human cognition; and (3) going beyond human cognition.

I like to think about AI as a mountain – a mountain where the upslope is "approaching human cognition" – the peak is "reaching human cognition" – and the downslope is "going beyond human cognition."

When we talk about human cognition, we talk about it as having two different parts: intelligence and consciousness.

It's important to keep in mind that biological intelligence and consciousness are not the same as machine intelligence and consciousness. This is because a machine is simulating the intelligence and consciousness of a biological entity.

I don't want to get too nerdy here, but it could be that there are other forms of intelligence and consciousness that we don't know about or understand. But what we're doing with the machines we are making is simulating human intelligence and human consciousness.

There is one more distinction to make when you are thinking about this, and that involves the concept of "simulation." Perhaps the best way to understand the difference between what is real in the physical world, and what is simulated, is through the following example.

I can run a simulation on a computer that simulates a black hole with a powerful gravitational pull. I can literally run the simulation on my laptop and watch it pulling all kinds of matter, including planets, into the black hole – anything that gets within the event horizon. But, it is not drawing me into the black hole because it is not real in the physical world – it is only real in the world of simulation. It is not creating the exact cause and effect it would create in the physical world – it is not pulling me into the computer and into that black hole.

So when we simulate intelligence and consciousness, we are not automatically creating biological intelligence and consciousness. We are creating a simulation of intelligence and consciousness.

I studied philosophy at one point in my early years, so I am positive that I have just violated a number of arguments one could make about simulations and reality. I won't go any deeper on this, but I do know it is important to keep in mind the difference between what is commonly observed as real versus simulated.

And there is another aspect to this. One could argue: "Well, what if you built a biological entity and put a simulated intelligence and consciousness within that biological entity? Is that entity then human or is it a simulated human?" Although this is an interesting question, I think it is beyond the scope of our discussion at the moment. I will say that by the time we do another edition of this book, we will likely have to deal with this question.

Types of AI

Let's return to the mountain analogy to help us understand and discuss types of AI.

Approaching human cognition is the upslope.
The peak is human cognition. And the
downslope is beyond human cognition.

Let's start with Automation. I think the jury is
split on whether automation is truly AI. That
would mean that we are still on the valley floor
and haven't begun to ascend the mountain yet.
We'll come back to this later though.

Automation is where you tell the software or
machine precisely what to do – "if this, then
that" instructional programming. This is hard
and tedious work to do, but defined this way,
we saw automation back in the Industrial Age
– where, for example, in textiles, we had
machines doing the human task of knitting and
weaving cloth. Humans had to design the
machine to do exactly what we wanted it to do.
Again, there are no perfect definitions, but I
think this is the cleanest way to define
automation for our terms.

Next is Robotics, where the robot is the machine – so now a robot is doing the human task. Robots usually have an element of mobility to them – a moving arm, or the device moving around on wheels, or simulated human legs.

Robots can be instructionally designed – "if this, then that" programming – or can be of the learning-type. If it is a non-learning robot, it is probably just beginning the upslope climb, at the same stage as automation; but if it is a learning robot, it is just ahead of the non-learning robot and automation.

Then we move to Machine Learning (ML). This is where the machine is teaching itself – the reason for the name machine learning. The machine, which can be hardware or software, learns to improve its algorithms through various methods, but almost all the methods involve feeding the ML a lot of data, continuously.

You are familiar with this type of AI if you pay attention to spam filters. When you tell your email system that something is spam, it learns from what you tell it – messages with those characteristics are then sent directly to your spam folder. The recommendation engines at Amazon or Netflix work the same way. They learn from your buying habits, viewing habits, and ratings.

I'm sure when you've tried to do some things online, you've encountered a mosaic of pictures and have been asked to click on the ones with cars in them. What you are being asked to do is label the pictures with cars in them to prove that you are not a robot. Besides doing that, you are telling an AI what pictures with cars in them look like. The AI can then use your labeling of cars to later distinguish cars better in some other applications.

Those of you who are thinking ahead of me, have probably already concluded that some good AI programmer could write an algorithm to automatically click on the pictures with cars in them – and there goes that "are you a human or a robot" test! Some refer to these types of AI as "Bots" – a "software robot." A bot is performing a human task, but it is software instead of hardware.

At this point, you're probably asking about Chess, Go, and Jeopardy!-winning AIs. These are forms of what is called "narrow AI." This is where the AI algorithms can do something better than a human can. As we've discussed earlier, this has already happened in playing Chess and Jeopardy!, and more recently in playing Go. One could argue that narrow AI has been with us for quite a while, because a simple calculator can exceed what most humans can do, or at least do it quicker.

The next step up the slope is Deep Learning (DL). This is a form of machine learning where problems are broken into pieces, and algorithms are run in parallel to get to the answer quicker than if you had to run them sequentially. The distinguishing characteristics of a DL AI are where you can break the problem into pieces, and you can get a lot of data to feed the algorithm.

Advanced robotics incorporate a form of machine learning in them. These are the robots you see that scramble around buildings and up stairs. The robot senses the environment, takes that data and goes through the process of teaching itself how to function within what it has sensed.

So, the more sophisticated the sensing, the more advanced the physical robot and its mobility, the more sophisticated the algorithms, and the more relevant the data you can feed it, the more likely the robot is able to do amazing things.

This is a tall order, which is the reason so many robots are limited in function, or are partnered with humans to accomplish things – such as the military drones of today.

The most sophisticated AI we see today is an example of Deep Learning AI (DL AI) – and that is self-driving cars. You teach the AI by having a human drive and collect sensing data. You've broken the driving process into hundreds of pieces, and created sensors for each of the pieces. The AI then observes the human's reactions to situations, and through that, it learns the right thing to do. After enough situations, the DL AI can take the wheel with the human observing and correcting. And after a while, enough situations, and enough data, the DL AI can drive the car.

Deep Learning AI is probably half-way up the slope of AI, depending on how complicated the application. If it is facial recognition or voice recognition, it is lower down – mostly because they are fairly narrow in scope. But if it is driving a car – where the scope of activity is getting broader – it is probably mid-way up the slope.

So, as mentioned earlier, with one of the most sophisticated applications of AI we see today – the self-driving car – I think we are only half-way up the AI mountain.

That means we have a long way to go before we reach human cognition – the ability to do everything a human does. Until we see applications with the scope of self-driving cars pervade almost everything we do, we are not approaching the peak of the mountain – at least in my view.

So what is this peak of the mountain – the equivalent of human cognition? It is simulating human intelligence in all areas. That is where the AI is not just able to drive a car as well as a human can, but it is able to do everything a human being can do. This is called "Artificial General Intelligence," or AGI.

Then have the downslope – called "Superintelligence." And this is where the AI goes beyond the abilities of a human being, in all ways.

A final complication is the question of consciousness. There is a split in thinking on whether human consciousness needs to be part of the definition of human cognition, or human abilities. After a lot of thought on this, for our purposes, I think the question is too complicated for this discussion. But, as I've mentioned a few times before, it probably will be important to discuss by the time I write the second edition of this book.

The more practical question is, when do we think we will reach the peak of the mountain – this AGI?

Well, I will tell you that there are three answers to that question – the most optimistic, the common view, and then my view.

The most optimistic view is held by Elon Musk, Ray Kurzweil, and a handful of others, who believe human-level AGI will be with us during the 2020s.

A common view of those working in the field is that we will see AGI around 2060 or so – 40 to 50 years from now.

And there are plenty of highly respected experts who think it will be by the year 3000 or later before we see human-level AGI.

I think the real answer is that we just don't know. And, I do not see the evidence to support that we will see AGI in the next 20 years or so – and I study this stuff every day. There is a lot a work going on in AI, with centers of excellence at the University of Toronto, MIT, Stanford, and other prestigious institutions around the world – not to mention the work going on at Google, Microsoft, Baidu, and IBM, to name a few. But I don't see the glimmers of hope that would put the number before 2080 to 3000.

Self-driving car AI is probably the most advanced we have today, but there are two other highly-useful applications of AI – image recognition and speech recognition. So let's close our discussion of AI by doing a quick experiment to show the current capabilities of a pretty sophisticated speech recognition AI application – Siri.

If you ask Siri a question like this: "Who won the London marathon in 1981?" The first answer you will get directs you to a website with information about the London Marathon. If you persist in your questioning, you'll finally be told that there was a tie in 1981 between Dick Beardsley and Inge Simonsen.

If you then ask a follow-up question like, "How many legs did she have?", it will fail miserably – or in more common words, choke. It will choke because it doesn't have the context of the original question still in its simulated mind – "Who won the London Marathon in 1981". The answer you'll get is a list of websites that describe how many legs a lot of things have. And, if you again persist and ask the question a second time, like I just did, you get an answer like: "Interesting question."

The point here is this: human cognition and intelligence are complex. It's not clear what human intelligence really is. We know how the human brain works chemically and electrically, but we still don't understand how intelligence works. Some think it may be pattern recognition, but there is a long way to go to sort this out.

And think about the two Siri-London Marathon questions – not really hard for humans. But the intricacies of the second question are hard for the AI of today – and a pretty sophisticated AI at that.

Turing Test

I will end our discussion of AI with this – the Turing test. The Turing test, developed by Alan Turing in 1950, holds that when we cannot distinguish between the intelligent behavior of a machine and that of a human, the machine has reached human equivalence.

We will need to see machines demonstrating human equivalence across the vast areas of human behavior before we start getting close to AGI.

Chapter 9 – AI and the Digital Platform

So why have we taken this trip through AI?

I think it's the technology we need to keep our eye on, the one that we need to understand as best we can, because I think it will be the technology of the future. And I hope that by now you agree.

But you have every right to ask, "Okay, but look – data analytics, cloud computing, blockchain, quantum computing – aren't they important too?"

And I would say, absolutely, they are important. But to me, data analytics, cloud computing, blockchain, and quantum computing are all parts of that digital platform we've built. They are aspects of it. But I think AI is going to be the enabler of our future world, the technology that will help us use this digital platform that we've built and use it well, meaning protect it and allow us to use it for productive means.

So, let's go back to Einstein's quote, "Logic will get you from A to B, but imagination will take you everywhere." We need to be constantly imagining where technology is going, and what the positives and negatives will be. But then we need always to bring it back to "what do we need to be doing today and tomorrow to get from A to B."

Let me give you one idea to think about – an idea that I'm thinking hard about. We've built this digital platform that we now function on, both personally and professionally. One of the key negatives is attacks on that platform by bad actors. Today, they use simple methods for their attacks, but it is reasonable to expect them to use AI to help in these attacks at some point in the future.

Wouldn't it be wise for us to begin a serious effort to use AI to protect our digital platform? And, in doing that, we might even learn how to control the power of AI development, so we don't have to be so concerned about it getting out of hand at some point – and we humans falling under its mercy.

Chapter 10 – The Digital Age?

I will end with this question: Are we living through a new age?

Are we living through one that is comparable to the Agricultural Age or the Industrial Age?

Are we living through the Digital Age?

I'll leave that for you to answer.

References

Agrawal, A., Gans, J., & Goldfarb, A. (2018). *Prediction Machines: The Simple Economics of Artificial Intelligence*. Boston, MA: Harvard Business Review Press.

Bostrom, N. (2014). *Superintelligence: Paths, Dangers, Strategies* (First edition). Oxford, United Kingdom: Oxford University Press.

Domingos, P. (2015). *The Master Algorithm: How the Quest for the Ultimate Learning Machine Will Remake Our World*. New York, NY: Basic Books.

Kurzweil, R. (2005). *The Singularity Is Near: When Humans Transcend Biology*. New York, NY: Viking.

Tegmark, M. (2017). *Life 3.0: Being Human in the Age of Artificial Intelligence* (First edition). New York, NY: Alfred A. Knopf.

Index

"

"I know you're lying because your lips are moving.", 56

2

2001, 55

A

Access, 38, 39, 42, 43, 57
AGI, 71, 72, 73, 76
Agricultural Age, 15, 16, 17, 19, 20, 22, 23, 27, 34, 80
Agricultural Revolution, 15
AI, 11, 12, 32, 33, 40, 57, 58, 60, 63, 64, 66, 67, 68, 69, 70, 71, 73, 75, 77, 78, 79
Airbnb, 29
Alan Turing, 75
algorithms, 65, 67, 68
Amazon, 34, 66
Apple, 10, 33
approaching human cognition, 60
arithmetic, 59
Artificial General Intelligence, 71
artificial intelligence, 11, 12, 32, 53, 87
Artificial Intelligence, 1, 40, 53, 87
ATM, 9, 10, 11, 24, 25
Automation, 64

B

Baidu, 73
banking, 24, 25, 27
BI, 40
big data, 40
Bill Gates, 29
bitcoin, 51
black hole, 62
blockchain, 77
Board of Directors, 5
Bots, 67
Business Intelligence, 40
business model, 8, 10, 23, 24, 27, 28, 29, 34

C

cellular network, 41
central processing unit, 59
CEO, 5, 6, 87
CFO, 5
Chess, 67
CIO, 5, 49
CISO, 49
Classical Computing, 59
cloud computing, 30, 32, 77
Columbia University, 5, 87
connectivity, 27, 39
consciousness, 56, 61, 62, 63, 71
conversion, 31
Conversion, 31
CPU, 59
CTO, 5, 49
CUSS framework, 48
cybersecurity, 53, 54
Cybersecurity, 1, 87

D

E

F

G

H

I

J

Y

Y2K, 13

Vecker Project

Please visit my website www.vecker.com and join us as a member of the Vecker Project, where every month, we address a new technology topic with a presentation, videocast, and resource information – to help you navigate these murky but exciting waters of technology.

About the Author

Thomas Cowan now makes his home at Columbia University. This follows the first half of his career at IBM and the second half building software companies.

Tom rose through the leadership ranks to become CEO, Board Director, and Chairman of ten companies and boards of directors, including public, private, non-profit, and academic organizations.

Today, Tom's focus is on the digitization of our society, artificial intelligence, and the paths forward.

He has served on many boards, including OutlookSoft, Tivoli, Tagetik, PGA.com, and NHL.com. He has chaired audit, compensation, governance, and nominating committees. Tom has also been Executive in Residence at RockRidge Capital Partners.

Tom is currently Associate Director of the Center for Technology Management and on the faculty at Columbia University. He also serves as board director and chairman for several technology companies and is an advisor to investment firms and technology CEOs.

His latest book, published in November 2018, is *Leading in the Digital Age: Disruption, Transformation, Data, Cybersecurity, Artificial Intelligence*. Tom's academic background includes undergraduate work at Wake Forest University, an MBA from the University of South Carolina, and doctoral studies at Columbia University.

www.ingramcontent.com/pod-product-compliance
Lightning Source LLC
LaVergne TN
LVHW041218050326
832903LV00021B/683